Beautiful
Oregon Country

Beautiful
Oregon Country

Concept and Design: Robert D. Shangle
Text: Brian Berger

First Printing November, 1979
Published by Beautiful America Publishing Company
P.O. Box 608, Beaverton, Oregon 97075
Robert D. Shangle, Publisher

Library of Congress Catalog Card Number
79-3847
ISBN 0-89802-091-3 paperback
ISBN 0-89802-092-1 hardbound

McCord Creek, Columbia Gorge

Cape Meares, Tillamook County

Contents

Beautiful America Publishing Company

The nation's foremost publisher of quality color photography

Current Books

Alaska, Arizona, British Columbia, California, California Vol. II, California Coast, California Desert, California Missions, Colorado, Florida, Georgia, Hawaii, Idaho, Los Angeles, Michigan, Michigan Vol. II, Minnesota, Montana, Montana Vol. II, Mt. Hood (Oregon), New York, New Mexico, Northern California, Northern California Vol. II, North Idaho, Oregon, Oregon Vol. II, Oregon Coast, Oregon Country, Pennsylvania, Portland, San Diego, San Francisco, Seattle, Texas, Utah, Virginia, Washington, Washington Vol. II, Washington D.C., Wisconsin, Yosemite National Park

Forthcoming Books

California Mountains, Illinois, Indiana, Kentucky, Las Vegas, Maryland, Massachusetts, Mississippi, Missouri, Nevada, New Jersey, North Carolina, Oklahoma, Ozarks, Rocky Mountains, San Juan Islands, South Carolina, Tennessee, Vermont, Wyoming

Large Format, Hardbound Books

Beautiful America, Beauty of California, Glory of Nature's Form, Lewis & Clark Country, Western Impressions

Photo Credits

Enlarged Prints

Most of the photography in this book is available as photographic
enlargements. Send self-addressed, stamped envelope for information.
For a complete product catalog, send $1.00.
Beautiful America Publishing Company
P.O. Box 608
Beaverton, Oregon 97075

Ritner Creek Covered Bridge, Peedee

Introduction

"To him who in the love of Nature holds
Communion with her visible forms, she speaks
A various language."

William Cullen Bryant
Thanatopsis

In writing the words quoted above, Bryant echoed what the Indians of early Oregon already knew—that nature has a language of her own. If one is attentive to her various moods, she will speak a universal tongue. It may be in the clear waters of a quiet stream cascading gently over protruding rocks. It may be in the breath of her winds, stirring autumn's leaves, or in the rain and the sounds of distant thunder. Whatever form she may choose, for those who will listen, she speaks an ageless truth.

Oregonians know nature's truth. For many it is her change of seasons with the land's exciting visual transformation. For others, it is the pounding of her surf and the sculptural forms of her coastline, carved by eons of relentless erosion. To others, it is the ice-covered masses of her volcanically-formed mountains, thrusting prominently above the Cascade Range. Or it could be the great forests of Douglas Fir, Ponderosa Pine and Western Hemlock, with their odors of oozing sap. It is the cut fields of golden wheat in Morrow, Gilliam, and Sherman counties, the red of ripening apples in the orchards of the Willamette Valley, the massing of great thunderheads, till their agitation gives forth life-giving rain. And it is in the streams and rivers, with the gem-like glint of a rainbow trout or the powerful tail thrusts of the chinook salmon as it fights the mighty current of the Columbia River. It is the winds of autumn, stripping the White Birch, Sugar Maple, and Oregon Ash of their colorful dress. It is the western meadowlark, the willow goldfinch, and the Oregon towhee, filling the air with their songs and bright colors. It is the subdued golden light of a late-afternoon sun, gilding the trees in the Columbia Gorge; and it is the Southeastern High Desert, humbling in its immenseness and solitude.

The words *Oregon* and *Nature* seem interchangeable. They reflect in their meaning all that Oregonians love about the wholesomeness of their green land, the liveability of their cities and townships, the sane tempo of their lifestyle—and an attitude toward keeping the Oregon of the future the same great place to live and work in that it is today. There is a "specialness" about Oregon that arouses her citizens to combat unnecessary encroachment in her forested areas. They rebel against the destruction of her historical "old towns" for the modern construction that would darken her streets and diminish the spacious feel of her cities. They guard against the pollution of her rivers, the infringement on her coastal areas by uncaring developers, and the influx of "too many" people trying to share what is *their* paradise.

But Oregonians *are* friendly people. Once assured that a sometime-visitor has firmly planted his heels, and is willing to enjoy the "real Oregon" on a yearly live-in basis, Oregonians loosen up. It is because they know that to *really* love Oregon is to love her year-round. It is not only to love her summers of colorful flowers, fun-filled days, aromatic evenings, and limitless greenery, but to love the colors of her autumn days, and the winds of her winters. It is to love the rain-laden clouds feeding her fertile lands, or carpeting the mountains with the white of their snows. It is to revel in the sounds of the ocean, as a storm sends her waves hard against the land, erupting in a foamy spray; to love all that is Oregon, and never to doubt that she is the best that nature has to offer.

Oregon's choice of recreation is legendary. It begins at her rugged coastline, offering state parks with all the conveniences, where fishing and clamming are popular pastimes, and continues to the Willamette Valley, where endless roads winding through colorful farm lands can take a visitor past her early settlements. The mighty Cascades, with many hiking trails cutting across the faces of these weather-worn giants, provide a platform *extraordinaire* for viewing the grandeur of the forests below. And in the vast area that is eastern Oregon, fishing and hunting top the list of favorite sports—this, and much more, forms the drawing card for her recreation.

It has been said, "Beauty soon grows familiar to the lover, fades in his eye, and palls upon the sense," but Oregonians' love for their land seems only to increase, as their ever-growing familiarity with its riches brings new wonderment at her diversity of climate, agricultural yield, wildlife, and spectacular beauty.

It must be said, then, that Oregon's "truth" is in all that her bountiful land has to offer to those lucky enough to have listened to her primordial call. For those who have heard only a distant whisper of that truth, there is an opportunity to visit and acquire a better understanding of her nature.

Brian Berger

Tumalo Falls, Deschutes National Forest
(Following pages) Mt. Jefferson, Mt. Jefferson Wilderness

Eastern Oregon

I f you were to ask the average visitor to Oregon how best to describe the state in terms of its environmental qualities, the answer most probably would be: "Its abundance of greenery, its lakes teeming with fish, and its mildness of climate . . . these are what Oregon means to me!" Of course, he would be right. Oregon is all this . . . but also something more!

That something more is *desert* . . . a vast lava plateau. Were it to be torn from the face of Oregon, it would leave a gaping hole one-quarter the size of the state. This is the Oregon desert, and it comprises most of Eastern Oregon, and sizeable chunks of Central Oregon down to the Oregon-California border. It is a land of total stillness by day, a desolate landscape of burning rock, treeless vistas of earth-torn faults and volcanic craters towering like giant anthills. Here, strong winds grasp its sands and fling them against massive rocky cliffs, eroding their craggy faces, and in time, forming sometimes-beautiful, sometimes-grotesque shapes in their huge outcroppings. By night, there is the cold, where the stillness (it seems) intensifies, but where, if one is quiet enough, can be heard the sandy stirrings and varied voicings of its nocturnal animal life. It is where the looming, volcanic shapes of the day blend in with darkness, or assume terrifying figures etched against a bright moonlit sky. While trying to grasp its enormous solitude, one can often hear the high-voiced, plaintive call of a distant coyote, filling the night's void with its haunting refrains.

"But wait," some will say, "this to me *is* Oregon!" They too will be right. For there is beauty here, a harsh, and sometimes frightful beauty that emerges as the vitality of its animal life, the sense-electrifying cleanness of its air, and the eye-saturating vivid colors of its morning and evening skies as they bleed against a brightening and fading canvas of blue. The colorful beauty of the dry-country plant life offers a study in the economy of the water-starved land; and the canyon cutting might of the Snake River, where it still flows free, displays a magnificence that is unexcelled.

Snake River looking north from Dry Diggins Lookout

Settlement in the eastern desert sections was slow in coming. Most Oregon-bound immigrants bypassed its formidable open vastness in favor of the longer, more hospitable route (if parts of the Oregon Trail at that time could be called hospitable) where it accompanied the Columbia River, and later cut through the Barlow Pass. It wasn't until 1863 that a few strong souls ventured into this sagebrush-infested openness, and even *they* did not gamble on making it in this easternmost sector, but headed instead to the area of Central Oregon where water flowed a little more freely and trees did not have to fight for a foothold. Today, the towns of Burns and Hines, two of the desert's largest, are by city standards fairly small. Nyssa and Ontario, located almost on the Oregon-Idaho border, and Vale, close by, comprise the balance of the most populated centers in this southeastern section, with Ontario's 8,950 nearly equalling the populations of the others, together!

There are other towns in this unending vastness, to be sure; but though their names are listed in the index of most Oregon maps, their population totals are not. It must be surmised then, that since 1863, it has taken a special love for this land to tempt those who would live in this Oregon desert to carve a life for themselves out of its beautiful and hardened landscape.

But there is another portion of Eastern Oregon: its northern section. Here the valley of the Grande Ronde River snuggles against the borders of the Blue Mountains on its western side and the heavily-forested slopes of the Wallowas on its east. The climate is different here; the rain that falls (and it falls with greater frequency than in the southeastern section) stays, and doesn't trickle away into alkalai deposits, or evaporate on contact. This is an area plentiful in streams and ripe with fish. And for those who have never tasted the might of a still wild canyon-forming river, the Snake—entering Oregon near the town of Adrian further south—follows the Oregon-Idaho border the balance of its northeastern side.

Eastern Oregonians are fortunate to still have one of the longest untamed stretches of the Snake skirting their province—the Hells Canyon run. There the river surges through a deep chasm, at times rushing a mile below its upper rim, where the curving walls of the gorge's lower levels obscure its near-vertical upper faces. A rafter is transported through a surreal world of reflecting light, and the warm colors of stratified rock.

Pendleton, La Grande and Baker are this area's largest cities, with Pendleton the home of one of Oregon's most famous rodeos—the Pendleton Round-Up. There are great vistas of wheat here, carpeting the Deschutes-Umatilla Plateau, extending from Pendleton to The Dalles. Their golden shafts bow to the wind's shifting currents. La

Abandoned farmhouse, Wallowa County

Grande, in the valley of the Grande Ronde River, absorbs the area's inflow of agricultural produce, lumber, and livestock, acting as a distribution point to distant markets for the products of Union and Wallowa counties. Baker, on the upper Powder River, achieved its early fame as a gold rush town after the discovery of "color" in Griffith Creek, just south of the city.

First to meet this both fertile and austere landscape of Eastern Oregon, the early settlers chose to bypass its varied beauty in favor of the tamer qualities of the Willamette Valley. But some retraced their steps, perhaps drawn back by strong tuggings of remembered beauty, perhaps by the need to test its harsher aspects against their own robust nature. Or perhaps, for a quality that defies mere definitions . . . a deep-felt yearning to explore its untapped excellence.

Wallowa Lake

Hells Canyon Overlook, halfway up Oregon rim

21

The Wallowa Range, Matterhorn at Sunset

Glacier Lake, Eagle Cap Mountain

Paulina Lake, Deschutes National Forest

The Oregon Coast

I magine, if you will, an almost straight stretch of land, averaging five miles in width, and extending from Brookings, close to the California border, to where Fort Stevens overlooks the mouth of the Columbia River at the northwestern-most tip of the state. A visitor traveling south along Highway 101, running through the middle of this narrow strip, would begin a journey of some 350 miles, down one of the most unspoiled and scenic shorelines in the United States . . . the Oregon Coast.

As romantic—and at times, as turbulent—as when Captain Vancouver first mapped part of its rugged beauty in 1792-94, the Oregon Coast holds a special attraction, both for visitors who have heard of its striking landforms, and for native Oregonians who have tasted its salty air and walked its many beaches. The small towns located near its inlets provide hours of browsing pleasure with their antique and gift shops. For those who love the feel of rolling water, sea excursions for the sightseer and charter-boat runs for the rod-and-reel crowd are offered by the day and hour. An abundance of clams finds rubber-booted afficionados—and bare-footed beginners—slogging over the low-tide sands, looking for a tell-tale sign of the entrenched whereabouts of these bivalves. Tide pools are a rich source of small sea-life for the curious, with sea urchin, sea cucumber, and occasionally, a purple starfish nestled in among the sea anemone—the ''flowers'' of these shallow, rock-enclosed gardens, which sway with the slight shiftings of their watery world.

Beachcombing is another favorite pastime. During the early-morning hours a lucky wanderer may find a glass float, washed up during the night, from the net of some far-off Japanese fishing vessel. Or perhaps one will encounter a unique piece of driftwood, its gnarled shape resembling a familiar profile or a favorite animal.

As exciting as these leisure-time activities are, they must come in only as a close second to the overwhelming scenic wonderland formed by the coast itself and its backdrop of lush vegetation—the Coastal Range. Here are miles of sandy shoreline, broken at intervals by the huge, rocky outcroppings of steep capes: Yaquina Head, Cape Lookout, Tillamook Head, and others. Giant walls of rock meet the fury of the

Sunset, Arch Cape
(Following pages) Crater Lake

winter ocean, bringing to mind the old question of what happens ''when an immoveable object meets an irresistible force.'' Here the battle seems a timeless one, but inevitably, the sea exerts the more telling force—and yearly claims its reward. The rays of a declining midsummer sun glisten off the curls of rolling surf and stretch to the waters of a distant horizon, laying an Oz-like path of undulating quicksilver. In the winter, the heavy fog is like a comforting blanket, hiding the seekers of solitude from all who would disturb their moment of introspection.

Before the Coast Highway was completed in 1932, a beach excursion was a less spontaneous occasion than it is today. The hearty traveler either had to trek in by foot through the Coast Range, or catch a ride with one of the coastal lumber schooners that frequented the few ports. When rails were finally laid—paralleling what is now US 101—travel was made easier by taking the Spokane, Portland, and Seattle Railroad, running between Astoria and Seaside; or the Southern Pacific Railroad, with routes between Mohler and Tillamook, and Reedsport and Coquille.

Thanks to modern ease of travel, the Coast Range no longer stands as a geographic barrier. But in many places the range is still the unblemished forest of an earlier day, and away from the highways the traveler can gain an impression of the land as it was a century ago. This low and rolling ridge of green hills stands back from the ocean from five to eight miles in some places, while in other areas it crowds close to the water, producing awesome cliffs and headlands. The range extends inland about 20-30 miles, smoothing out into the cultivated valleys of the interior. The Coast Range contains the richest of Oregon flora. In the dampness of the forest floor, clinging to fallen logs, grow the lace-like sword, deer and bracken ferns. Red huckleberry and elderberry add color to the cool greenness that surrounds the occasional Oregon myrtle, and the fragile cream-and-pink flowers of the western azalea. Tall conifers—mostly Douglas Fir, Grand Fir, Western Cedar, and Western Hemlock—stand like ancient pillars, supporting a canopy of interlacing greenery and providing the shade that traps the moisture needed for the verdant stretches of forest floor. When dusk comes, the glow of a swiftly vanishing sun appears to set the forest ablaze. As its still brilliant rays color the gathering clouds in hues of burning-gold, and wispy lines of smoky-reds, one is made to feel that he has just witnessed ''. . . a scene out of the classic period of the earth . . . .''

The temperature of the Oregon Coast is uniformly mild, with an annual average of about 50 degrees. The Pacific Ocean exerts a stabilizing influence on the region, resulting in mild winters and cool summers, while burdening the air with high moisture levels throughout the year. Heavy rains can be expected on 50 to 60 days of the winter months. Some areas receive as much as 100 inches annually, helping to

Heceta Head Lighthouse

perpetuate the myth of Oregon's liquid sunshine. But, abundant as the dampness is, summers are mostly free of the heavy and persistent stuff, resulting in warm temperatures—65 to 70 degrees—and pleasantly mild evenings, bringing beach-lovers in droves to enjoy the foamy surf and warm sands.

The history of the towns that hug the coast is as fascinating as that of the early settlements of the Willamette Valley. Rich in the lore of early sailing ventures, lumbering operations, and seekers after gold, the coastal towns have inspired many famous writers to write well-read novels. Jack London, staying for a while in Port Orford, finished part of his novel, *The Valley of the Moon;* and Joaquin Miller—the famous ''Byron of Oregon''—traveled to the same spot to marry Minnie Myrtle Dyer, of whom he had grown fond after reading her poetry.

Not surprisingly, Astoria—near the mouth of the Columbia River and a few miles inland from the coast—is steeped in historical drama. Here it was that Captain John Gray, negotiating the tricky passage from the Pacific into the Columbia's rushing and turbulent current, first sighted (in 1792) what was to become the first permanent settlement in present-day Oregon. Named in 1811 for John Jacob Astor, it became an important trading post, later falling into the hands of the British for a short time, and then reverting to the United States. In 1821, the fort was given to the command of Dr. John McLoughlin as Chief Factor, and subsequently abandoned as the headquarters for the Hudsons Bay Company in 1824, when they moved further inland to establish a new fort at Vancouver on the Washington side of the Columbia. The real settling of Astoria began in 1844, with the arrival of the early immigrants. It was soon to become the second largest city in the state, with fishing, logging, and canning its chief assets. Today, the city is still graced with many old structures of its past. Fishing and tourism remain important contributors to its economy.

Seaside, Cannon Beach, Tillamook, Lincoln City, Depoe Bay, and Newport are located on the coast's northern half. Waldport, Florence, Reedsport, Coos Bay, Port Orford, and Gold Beach are on its southern half. These are just some of the many cities that dot this popular resort area. For the traveler, they become stepping stones to a historical and fun-filled journey down its scenic pathway, bordered by the sometimes-seething Pacific on one side, and on the other, the lakes and forests of the Coast Range.

Southern Oregon

Of the many spectacular landforms that identify southern Oregon, few can match the geologic masterpiece that is Crater Lake. Formed by the collapsed cone of Mt. Mazama, a giant volcanic mountain, it now contains the pristine waters of ages of melted snows and accumulated rains. So clear is the water of this totally contained lake that light penetrating its famed indigo-colored depths reaches into more than 400 feet of its 2,000-foot depth.

The story of Crater Lake is one of countless ages of volcanic upheaval during which a mountain rose that matched the mighty peaks of today's Cascades. Its volcanic temper cooled, and this snow-capped giant (estimates run between 12,000 and 15,000 feet) lay dormant for thousands of centuries. Then, about 7,000 years ago, the sleeping giant awoke. The eons of slumber had not cooled its inner fires. Slowly at first, and then with mountain energy, ash, then pumice, spewed forth from its yawning crater. The great clouds of ash darkened the skies in an artificial night, and molten rock swept aside or burned everything in its path, with temperatures exceeding 2,000°C. When the earth ceased to tremble and the fires began to cool, the mountain's upper portion, deprived of its inner support, fell back into itself. What remained was a crater measuring six miles rim to rim, and 21 miles in circumference, the smoke from its still-hot interior emerging from the flooring 4,000 feet below.

Within recent times, further volcanic activity built a second mountain which rose from the interior of its cavity, to a height of 2,800 feet. Its top portion is now known as Wizard Island. Today, the clear waters that have filled this once-seething cauldron draw visitors by the thousands. An enjoyable drive around its rim on a well-paved road will afford the sightseer a chance to view the lake from several vantage points, while marveling at the beauty of its surrounding forest.

A second great body of water begins about 35 miles south of Crater Lake and extends to the northern boundary of the city of Klamath Falls. Known as Upper Klamath Lake, it is all that remains of an inland sea isolated by a chain of volcanoes formed near Oregon's coast 25 million years ago. Activity from these mountains over a 10-million year period eventually filled its flooring with deep lava flows,

Mt. Thielsen, Diamond Lake
(Following pages) Columbia Gorge

creating a giant lava plateau that these mountains now rest on. A haven for birds on their winter and summer migrations, the lake plays host to thousands of ducks, geese and migratory shorebirds. Perhaps the most famous of the many species are the white pelicans that soar gracefully over Klamath Falls and its environs.

Further west are the cities of Ashland, Medford, and Grants Pass, the first to welcome visitors as they cross the Oregon-California border on Interstate 5. Ashland is known nationwide for its annual Shakespearean Festival, which must rival in pageantry and verve the performances given by the Bard himself. Medford, established in 1883, began its growth in the 1850s with the influx of gold seekers, many staying to make this area their home after the yellow stuff disappeared. Medford is the largest city in this southwestern section, owing much to the fruit growing and lumber industry for its early, rapid expansion. Grants Pass, named after the famous General, was given its name by a party of road builders after Grant's success at Vicksburg. Mining provided its economic base in its early years, until lumber and agriculture became important forces.

One of the best fishing and recreational boating rivers in Oregon courses by the city of Grants Pass at its southern end, the Rogue. Famed for its sections of white water, the Rogue plunges down the western face of the Cascades from an area close to Crater Lake, and with relentless persistence—its waters fortified by the drainings of many tributaries—it rushes westward for its meeting with the Pacific. Given impetus by the 6,000-foot drop from the Cascades to the Rogue River Valley's north end, it seems not to slacken through the balance of its journey, churning into foamy, boat-tossing rapids in spots, all the while passing through areas of heart-pounding beauty.

About 200 million years ago, limestone deposits began a transformation and eventually turned into marble, imbedded in portions of the Siskiyou Mountains. Through untold ages, water, dripping into cracks in this easily-dissolved rock, formed holes that widened into the Oregon Caves. As the dripping water evaporated, it left tiny deposits of calcite which accumulated to form the cave's marvelous stalactite growths, which have fueled many a visitor's fantasy. Located 50 miles south of Grants Pass, these ''marble halls of Oregon'' were discovered in 1874 by a surprised hunter, who was trying to locate his dog. Entering a passage overgrown by vegetation, he struck a match and beheld what is now a popular tourist attraction.

Scenic hiking trails, swift-running streams plentiful in fish, great vistas of ice-capped mountains, lakes of snow-water freshness, and National Forests with numerous camping sites form the southwestern entrance to beautiful Oregon. They serve as a parting reminder to those fortunate enough to have spent their vacations here that they have shared in a supreme gift of nature.

Central Oregon

Central Oregon is a land of diverse geologic forms and climatic regions. If one could command a view of the whole of Oregon by attaining a sufficient altitude, he would quickly see the city of Bend at its center and portions of four climatic areas circling it: the rugged mountains of the High Cascades to its west, the Deschutes-Umatilla Plateau to its north, the mountains of the Northeastern Highlands, and east and south, the flatter lands of the Great Basin, or High Plateau country.

During the Triassic period of the Mesozoic Era (about 225 million years ago), warm seas covered this interior region, where today are found rich deposits of the fossilized remains of many of its marine inhabitants. Over millions of years there was a gradual uplifting of the floor of this sea, and with the recession of its waters it became a plain. An era of tremendous volcanic activity followed. Great flows of molten rock spewing from underground furnaces covered much of Central Oregon, leaving their land-building story in the forms of many volcanic cones that dot the area, and in the nearly mile-thick lava flows that blanket great portions of the landscape.

The High Cascades, acting as a barrier against the intrusion of marine air that dampens the western section of Oregon, limit the rainfall in parts of this region to as little as 10 inches or less per year. But in the higher elevations of its forested areas, rainfall reaches more plentiful levels, with the western face of the High Cascades accumulating 60 to 100 inches. The Cascades themselves rest on a great lava plateau, with the prominent peaks of its range built up by volcanic activity and sculpted by the glacial fields that covered most of its length in an earlier period.

If a circle were to be drawn around the Bend-Prineville area, one would find the counties of Jefferson, Crook and Deschutes entirely within the Central Oregon section, with parts of Wasco, Wheeler, Grant, Harney, Lake and Klamath intruding into its perimeter. One will find great extremes of temperature within this circle, with the cities of the High Plateau experiencing below-freezing conditions in the month of January; and in July, a dry heat approaching 100 degrees. But as harsh as this climatic variance sounds, Central Oregon is an ideal recreation and living area.

From the town of Prineville in Crook County, Highway 26 cuts through the Ochoco National Forest (843,694 acres) with its stands of juniper and pine. Here are 11 major campgrounds, many in an area offering exciting rock-hunting possibilities in what has been termed an "agate paradise." The spring runoff brings good fishing to its many streams, while for the hunter, mule deer, antelope, and elk make this a popular area for bagging the *big* ones.

The John Day Fossils Beds, located just northeast of Ochoco, are a geologic goldmine, first made famous by the early explorations of Oregon's first geologist, Thomas Condon. Condon found the area to be a treasure house of revealing vertebrate fossils, including a then-unique species of three-toed horse, *Miohippus condoni*. In writing to a friend about his diggings in the area, he commented on the problem he was having with the local bands of hostile Indians, "*.* . . (they compel me) to hold a rifle in one hand and a pick in my other."

Southwest of Prineville, the city of Bend, straddling the Deschutes River, is a thriving lumber community that also depends on agriculture for its economic well-being. Recreationally, Bend offers its 17,000 residents easy access to many lakes and streams within a 50-mile radius of its limits, and a chance at exploring the architecture of its volcanic past. Here, the pent-up energy of a still-forming crust has created ripples and high cones on its surrounding landscape—with names like Pilot and Lava Butte, and the Dillman Cave, a lava-formed tunnel located in Lava River Caves State Park. Additionally, the Arnold Ice Cave, 15 miles southeast of the city, is a frigid cavern of year-round sparkling splendor, where in the early days of Bend's history, its residents removed great chunks of its icy flooring, hauling the considerable weight of this ice by wagon, when the rivers nearby failed to freeze.

Bend does not experience the drier environment of communities located some distance to the southeast of it, due mainly to the plentiful supplies of water draining from the east face of the Cascades. Also, the abundance of its timbered lands harbors a greenness that provides for more pleasant forms of recreation (i.e. camping and water sports). Not so for other communities that rely heavily on irrigation for their farming. They face a constant threat of low water supplies. The water that does flow through the many irrigation channels must flow in great quantities to be effective, due to the highly porous nature of the soil and its rocky substrata.

The diversion of irrigation water from the Bend area helped the growth of two cities to the north of it: Redmond and Madras. Water gushing through the main irrigation ditch built by the Central Oregon Irrigation Company changed this dusty sage and juniper land to a farming oasis of thousands of acres. Madras, on the other hand, developed its irrigation network in spurts, not reaching its present-day levels

(Following pages) North and Middle Sisters, Scott Lake

until 1946, with the completion of the U.S. Bureau of Reclamation project, which was begun in 1938.

Taken in total, the Central Oregon area presents many faces to the traveler. There are steep slopes of the Cascades' eastern face, with their still-lush forests. There are shining lakes filled with the most willing of ''fryers.'' There are geologic hunting grounds to keep even the most ardent rockhound busy. There are the faulted and arid lands of the High Desert with its many volcanic buttes, and the multi-hued slopes of the Painted Hills, stained by their mineral deposits. And finally, there are the sagebrush vistas of its open range lands, and a climate at once extreme and life-sustaining. Lost in this totality of stark contrasts, a traveler will be consumed by the moods of its varied landscapes, amazed by the tenacity of its fauna, and made to respect the strengths of its early settlers—who carved from its volcanic flooring a new life!

Hillside Spires, near Dayville

One of Heavenly Twin Lakes, Sky Lakes Area

Videa Falls, Crater Lake National Park

The Willamette Valley

Bounded on its east and west by the Cascade and Coastal ranges, the fertile fields of the Willamette Valley spread 187 miles, from the Columbia River through the "heartland" of Oregon. Here, 70 per cent of the state's population play, build and harvest. It is here that the first settlers of what is now the State of Oregon found the paradise they had been seeking after the long-fought hardships of the Oregon trail.

One can say that the life-blood of this lush region is drawn from the waters of the Willamette River, fed from its sources in the Umpqua National Forest, and from its tributaries, which drain from the high Cascades and the Coastal mountains. Discovered in 1806 by William Clark, of the Lewis and Clark expedition, the river was known then by its Indian name, *Multnomah.* Captain Clark was amazed at the river's width, and believed that its origin might be as far away as the Gulf of California. A map printed in London in 1814 showed its source near the Great Salt Lake in Utah. Today, the Willamette serves more than 600 industrial plants near its banks, and provides the water that irrigates the great farmlands of the Valley. Additionally, gravel, in the millions of tons, is dredged from its bed to supply Oregon's highway departments and cement industry. The river also is a source of coho and chinook salmon for the sports and commercial fisherman.

The Willamette was not always the healthy river that it is today. As late as the early '50s, it had a pollution problem of such vast proportions that it was called, ". . . the filthiest waterway in the Northwest, and one of the most polluted in the nation," by a state official. The river ran with raw sewage, wood residues, chemicals from the pulp and paper industry, and the garbage of food processors. Its native fish species could not survive the low oxygen levels caused by excessive bacteria, and fall chinook died as they tried to pass through Portland's harbor.

But it is a tribute to the people of Oregon—with their love for a healthy environment—that less than 10 years after realizing the magnitude of the problem, the waterway once again was a place for enjoying a refreshing summer's swim, waterskiing, or pulling the "big ones" from its clean depths. Strong, new anti-pollution laws were passed and the old ones strengthened. Pulp and paper mills were

Mt. Washington and Big Lake

Multnomah Falls, Columbia Gorge

made to install secondary waste-treatment facilities and chemical recovery units. Hot waste water was piped to nearby vegetable fields, increasing crop production. Tough standards were set for the quality of an industry's liquid discharges. Today, a watchful river patrol keeps potentially harmful mistakes from ever becoming the problem they once were.

It is predicted that by the year 1990, the population of the Willamette Valley will increase from its present figure of 1,541,000 to approximately 2,109,000. The same year, recreational uses of its rivers and parklands will increase by 100 per cent —from today's 8 million to 16 million. Because of the expected growth in recreation usage, and because Oregonians felt a need to set goals to further improve this economic and pleasure waterway, a plan was proposed in 1967 to begin the Willamette Greenway Project. The plan called for developing and maintaining ''. . . a natural, scenic, historical, and recreational Greenway . . . on lands within 150 feet from ordinary low water line . . . (including) all islands, State Parks, and recreation areas along the river . . . .'' The project as envisioned did not begin until 1975, and only after a number of years of controversy over just *what* areas would be affected. Because most of the land along the course of the river is in private ownership, and because each municipality has control over the laws governing the usage of land in its own areas, the project has never really materialized as first envisioned. What *has* taken place, though, is a keener awareness on the part of industry as to their role in helping to keep this river a viable waterway. The cities that depend so much on its commerce and recreational aspects will never again allow a lowering of pollution standards that would defile its waters.

At the northernmost end of this watery life-line, where it joins with the Pacific-bound current of the mighty Columbia River, spreads the City of Roses—Portland. Situated on both the east and west banks of the Willamette, Portland, with a population of 367,000, and its suburbs, contain the state's greatest density of residents. Here it was that in 1844, a man by the name of William Overton traded his share of a 640-acre tract (that was later to become Portland's west bank) for $100 in provisions and a 25-cent filing fee. It all came about when Overton, having cleared a small area fronting the river, found he lacked the 25 cents needed for filing his claim; so he offered *half* of the claim to Bostonian Amos L. Lovejoy if he would pay the hefty sum. Being the shrewd businessman that Lovejoy obviously was—he paid!

But Overton wasn't through giving away the future Portland yet. Deciding that Lovejoy's plan for building a town on the site would never materialize, he approached Francis W. Pettygrove (a Portland, Maine merchant) and offered to trade the balance of his acreage for the above-mentioned provisions. By 1845, having cleared 16 blocks, Pettygrove and Lovejoy decided they needed a name for the town, Lovejoy wanting the name "Boston," and Pettygrove holding out for Portland. They tossed a coin—and the rest is history.

Today Portland ranks as one of the "most liveable cities in the United States" (according to a report by the Midwest Research Institute), and most Portlanders would agree; however, they would rather not talk about it around "outsiders." Try as they may to hide it, Portland's "secret" is difficult to conceal. One has only to travel through the city from any direction, and its benefits become obvious. The hills form a green backdrop for the inner-city that rises along its west waterfront. Portland's residents face a magnificent vista crowned by Mt. Hood, its white-capped peak towering above the landscape, presenting an ever-changing spectacle of colors and shadow-patterns across its craggy face. Here too can be seen the distant countryside, where slow-moving clouds create a panorama of shifting lights over its surface, molding subtle changes in its form. The Willamette River winds its way under a network of bridges, glittering as the sun's late afternoon rays reflect from a million small ripples. Then, with night sweeping across the valley, the man-made sparkle of colored reflections from thousands of windows sets the evening's mood. Or perhaps one might drive to its eastern portion, where the city gradually blends into the greenery of the Columbia Gorge, with its many parks and sparkling blue waterfalls. The Columbia River provides watersports for those who camp along its many park-strewn miles. Its surging, dam-tapped might supplies 80 per cent of the Northwest's electrical power.

Yes, Portland is a beautiful city. But it is only one of the many populated areas of the Willamette Valley offering handsome working and living conditions. A visitor wanting to trace the historical wanderings of the Willamette River, where the early settlements lining its course have grown into prospering cities, might board a boat in Portland, and by traveling upriver eight miles, come abreast of the city of Lake Oswego. Named for Oswego, New York, in 1847 by the pioneer A.A. Durham, this thriving community of 21,700 surrounds the placid waters of Oswego Lake, a 3½-mile reservoir serving as a private recreation waterway for the many residents' houses along its tree-lined shores. Here too is a small artists' colony, with local galleries exhibiting examples of artistic creativity. The Festival of Arts (the climax of their gifted labor), with judging and monetary awards, is an annual event.

Continuing upstream, we come upon Oregon City. Its main center of activity is situated along the river's east bank. This town of 15,000 people has a wealth of firsts on its record regarding the Oregon country: the first territorial capital (1843); the

Willamette Valley from Mt. Angel

North Falls, Silver Falls State Park
(Following pages) Deschutes River at Sunriver

first sawmill and gristmill powered by water; the first United States flag unfurled; the first Protestant Church; the first Masonic Lodge; the first newspaper to be printed west of the Missouri River; the first brass band; the first mint; and the first paper mill. At this point on the Willamette, a long, basaltic ledge forms a series of steps over which the river drops 42 feet. Before 1869, river navigation encountered problems at Oregon City, due to low water levels. A number of locks were constructed on the east side of the falls, permitting even large vessels to navigate this difficult point.

Visitors to Oregon City will find McLoughlin House—moved from its former site at Third and Main Streets to McLoughlin Park—an interesting historical highlight. McLoughlin, who retired at Oregon City, and lived in the structure from 1846 until his death in 1857, was the Chief Factor of Fort Vancouver on the Washington side of the Columbia River. Working for Hudson's Bay Company, he controlled the fur trade in the area that reached from the Rocky Mountains as far as the Pacific Ocean, and from Alaska to California.

Following the river a little further brings us to Champoeg Memorial State Park—the site of the first settlement in the Willamette Valley. A flood destroyed the town in 1861, and no effort was never made to rebuild it. In 1900, the site was designated an historical landmark, and 107 acres were set aside as a state park. Two historical museums are located within the park, and plenty of picnic space is available for large groups to enjoy its well-maintained grounds.

Newberg is the next largest town after leaving Oregon City (population 10,000). Named by Sebastian Brutsher, for his home in Neuberg, Germany (and given the English spelling of the word) the town was founded by Quakers, and was the first settlement of its kind west of the Rocky Mountains. George Fox College—originally Pacific Academy—was built here in 1885 and has the distinct honor of having had Herbert Hoover, former President of the United States, as a member of its first graduating class, in 1888.

Departing from the river's course and heading overland about 15 miles in a southeasterly direction, we reach the community of Woodburn. The town founder, Jesse H. Settlemeier, started his fortune in the nursery business (later to become the largest nursery on the west coast) after moving to the area in 1862. Here he purchased 80 acres of land, where he built a log cabin on the present site of the town. Today, Woodburn provides its population of 11,500 with the peaceful qualities of its earlier lifestyle, while enticing new firms into its industrial park served by the Southern Pacific Railroad. Parks and a modern school system, together with its proximity to major population centers, have made Woodburn an attractive place to locate a growing family.

Fireweed, Upper Clackamas River

About 12 miles east of Woodburn, on State 211, is the small farming and lumbering community of Molalla. Known statewide for its yearly rodeo—the Molalla Buckaroo—the town saw its first settler in 1840. Feyrer County Park, located three miles southeast of town, offers 40 picnic sites with wood stoves, and a chance to fish and swim in the clear Molalla River.

Turning southwest on Highway 213, we head back in the direction of the Willamette, toward the town of Silverton. Named for the sparkling waters of Silver Creek that flow through the town, this early settlement's growth owed much to a sawmill that was built here in 1846. A famous resident was Silverton Bobbie, a dog made famous in a novel by Charles Alexander—*Bobbie, a Great Collie.* When taken east in 1926, the dog was lost in Indiana. Bobbie successfully found his way back to his old haunts, and the story deals with this amazing journey.

While in the area, a visit to Silver Creek Falls State Park (about 10 miles southeast on Highway 214) is a must. Nine waterfalls within its boundaries afford the visitor a spectacular display of their cool, mist-forming elegance. Several drop nearly 200 feet.

Taking Highway 14 to State 22, we arrive in Salem and are back with the Willamette. Its winding course runs through the western section of the city. As Oregon's capital city, Salem reflects all that is special about the State. Here we notice the uncluttered skyline and plaza-like feel, when walking about its historically rich streets. It is a feeling of "small-townness" that is pervasive in even the largest of Oregon's cities. There is a profusion of greenery shading its residential streets, and the aromas of rich and spicy foodstuffs offered by the colorful street-corner vendors. Here too are art galleries with their canvases that catch the mood of the local scene or the sweeping grandeur of the multi-hued Oregon countryside. The grand old houses, restored and redecorated, show the pride Salem's residents have for their historic heritage. One sees parks and landscaped plazas bright with spring's first flowers, and in the fall, one feels the winds as they whip gold and reddish leaves in a wild frenzy—their once-moist surfaces now scurrying withered about the streets. And there is the rain, familiar to Oregonians, washing the streets and land with its life-giving coolness.

The State Capitol building is Oregon's third on the same site. Two predecessors were destroyed by fire. The present structure was completed in 1938, constructed of white Danby Vermont marble. Atop its tower, a 24-foot figure representing "The Oregon Pioneer" stands shining—a result of 40 ounces of gold leaf coating its surface. Graced with the sculpures of Leo Friedlander at its front entrance—depicting "Lewis and Clark led by Sacajawea"—and the beautiful murals of Barry Faulkner

and Frank Schwarz lining its rotunda, the Capitol is a showcase of art, and a testament to the taste of its architect, Francis Keally, and the legislature that authorized its construction.

The early name for Salem was *Chemeketa,* meaning "resting place"—and it says a lot for the feel of the city today. Salem services a trade area of some 225,000 people, with agriculture and State government being its major employers. The area surrounding Salem, the mid-Willamette Valley, produces over 100 different crops, with gross sales in 1978 totaling an estimated $173 million.

Monmouth, a short distance southwest of Salem, is a farming community that is known for its purebred sheep and dairy cattle, and for the Oregon College of Education—where many of Oregon's teachers have trained—located in park-like surroundings. The town, established in 1853 on 640 acres of land, takes its name from Monmouth, Illinois, having been settled by emigrants from the area.

What becomes apparent to the traveler as he continues south is that these Willamette flat-lands were indeed a "Garden of Eden" to the weary seeker of a new land. Its rich alluvium-filled plains, combined with moderate climatic conditions, afforded the raising of any number of crops. The streams draining into the Willamette River—sources of water for the many farms that were to develop into Oregon's second largest industry—were plentiful with fish. The forests rising from the foothills of the Cascades and Coastal ranges offered the material to construct the many dwellings that would later mark the sites of its growing cities. The breast-high grasses nourished the first cattle herds, allowing summer and winter pasture on its virgin prairies. All of these combined to make the Willamette Valley the perfect home for the "seekers of paradise." It would be difficult for the visitor passing through this valley not to feel much the same stirrings in the blood that the early settlers must have experienced as they gazed upon its manifold gifts.

Now with a heightened sense of wonderment coloring his journey, the traveler finds that his passage upriver has brought him abreast of Albany, the seat of Linn County. Lumber products and food-processing plants are the leading industries in Albany, adding to the monies of the economy. Along the way the traveler is greeted by willows and cottonwoods gracing the riverbanks. As he nears Corvallis, the dark-green fields of mint and the red of harvested beets make their showing. Corvallis is the home of Oregon State University, known for its science, agricultural, and engineering programs. Through its Federal Extension Service Program, it offers information and services to farmers and those interested in home economics. First settled in 1845 and officially platted in 1851, the city has numerous points of interest for the history buff.

Barn and pond near Dallas

A light breeze stirs the maidenhair ferns along the riverbanks. The sun's rays dapple the grasses with the movements of restless leaves, and the hours pass without one being aware of it as the Springfield-Eugene area comes into sight. The traveler heads into the final leg of his journey. With a population of 104,000, Eugene is the second-largest city in the state and home of the University of Oregon. Add to the population the 42,000 residents of the Springfield area (a stone's throw away) and it becomes an important link in the lifeline of the valley's commerce. Its citizens are blessed with so many possibilities for recreation, it is hard to imaging anyone staying home for lack of something to do on weekends. Aside from its own historical pathways—providing one with pleasurable and informative afternoon walks within the city proper—there are the great National Forests of the Cascades. Here one will be drawn by the many lakes and streams—shaded by Douglas and Grand Fir and interspersed with western hemlock and red cedar. Ladies-tresses and the creeping buttercup mix with lady, maidenhair, and sword-ferns in the wet undergrowth. The air is filled with the pungent odors of new life emerging, and the old decaying in an ageless cycle on the forest's floor.

The Oregon Coast is a leisurely hour-and-fifteen-minute drive away, for beachcombing and souvenir hunting. Charter boats are available for offshore fishing. The Siuslaw National Forest of the Coast Range has fish in abundance, while hiking, horseback riding, and camping allow one to become familiar with the magnificence of its scenery.

All told, the Willamette Valley is indeed the Eden envisioned by its first settlers, providing jobs for the majority of Oregon's population, recreation of unlimited quantity and quality, liveable city environments, educational systems equalling the best in the country, and the opportunity for its citizens to commune daily with the ever-changing panorama of nature at their very doorsteps.

Olallie Lake
(Following page) Columbia Gorge Sunset